Exercise
Gratitude
Daily! ♡

Sharon & Luanne

The 28 Day Gratitude Workout

Exercises to Make EVERY Day Count!

Contact Us:

grateful@the28daygratitudeworkout.com
www.the28daygratitudeworkout.com

Connect with us on social media!

Facebook:
www.facebook.com/The28DayGratitudeWorkout
www.facebook.com/SharonItForwardToday
www.facebook.com/LSaragaWalters
www.facebook.com/MyVideoVoice

Twitter: @LouanneWalters

LinkedIn:
www.linkedin.com/in/LouanneSaragaWalters

Table of Contents

Table of Contents Continued

We dedicate this book to our parents, Frieda and Leonard Saraga, and Bob and Carol Walters. Thank you for creating us and raising us to always look for the good things in life!

INTRODUCTION

"True happiness is to enjoy the present, without anxious dependence upon the future, not to amuse ourselves with either hopes or fears but to rest satisfied with what we have, which is sufficient, for he that is so wants nothing. The greatest blessings of mankind are within us and within our reach. A wise man is content with his lot, whatever it may be, without wishing for what he has not." — *Seneca*

Welcome to The 28 Day Gratitude Workout - Exercises to make EVERY day count!

Louanne and I are so grateful you're committing to really building your gratitude muscle. When you do that - anything can happen!

It's said that a habit can be built in three weeks - we've added a fourth to anchor the experience. Over 28 days, you will do 28 different exercises designed to generate a greater awareness of all the good in your life. It might be within you, the value of others, the blessings in your work, home, family, the good you having flowing in your material life.

Gratitude works in **every** area of our lives, and its benefits start **immediately**. We all have different areas that are easier for us to be more grateful for - and areas in our lives we struggle to find any good. The exercises in this course are designed to cover a wide array of these areas - to give us practice in them all. If you find some that are particularly challenging, be grateful! You've just discovered an area of potential growth! See how this works?

Each day is its own chapter, and each chapter includes a section you can use to make note of any significant lesson or aha moment you've experienced in that exercise.

To really benefit from this workout, make it a personal commitment. Only you can benefit — or not - from being true to your daily exercises. If you miss a day, re-start by repeating the last day you had done and get back into the flow.

When you've finished this workout, repeat it again in order of the days 1-28, or choose a category you might want to work a little bit more on.

For example, if you want to focus on your gratitude toward others, choose the Make Someone's Day chapters. If you want to focus on your awareness of the good in your life, choose the 'Take Time to Notice' exercises.

Appendix A lists the exercises by week and day.
Appendix B lists the exercises by category.
Appendix C is an additional copy of each day's exercise so you repeat this workout.

THANK YOU for taking this course - we'd love to hear from you! Please visit us on our website and let us know how it's going.

www.the28daygratitudeworkout.com

Are you ready to start The 28 Day Gratitude Workout-
Exercises to Make EVERY Day Count?!

In Gratitude,
Sharon and Louanne Saraga Walters

DAY 1:
MAKE SOMEONE'S DAY

This exercise strengthens your ability to see the good and valuable in yourself and others.

"When we give cheerfully and accept gratefully, everyone is blessed." — *Maya Angelou*

We're going to ease into our 28 Day Gratitude Workout with a two step exercise.

Step 1:

Start by giving yourself three to five compliments. Say them out loud. They might be about a skill you've developed or a talent you have, or something you've accomplished recently, or about your hair or body - the point is to notice, acknowledge and compliment yourself.

You might find that this is outside of your comfort zone. That's ok - just commit to the exercise.

Step 2:

Compliment others throughout the day - your family members, neighbors, co-workers, even strangers.

Take special notice of those you might otherwise walk past. Bank tellers, clerks, receptionists, the people at check out registers, or bagging your groceries.

As you compliment them - visualize how your words might uplift them, and what good they in turn, can pass on.

It feels good, and makes you and them happy, and happy is a healthy state!

Happiness generates healthy endorphins, helps you think good thoughts, and change old thinking patterns. Exercise the muscle of noticing others and giving compliments and include yourself!

If it feels good, do it daily.

Day 1
MAKE SOMEONE'S DAY

Give yourself three to five compliments. Write them here and then say them out loud. They might be about a skill you've developed or a talent you have, or something you've accomplished recently, or about your hair or body - the point is to notice, acknowledge and compliment 3-5 things about yourself.

1.

2.

3.

Compliment others throughout the day - your family members, neighbors, co-workers, even strangers.

DAY 2:
TAKE TIME TO NOTICE

This workout is designed to increase your awareness
of the magnificence of the human body.

*"When you arise in the morning, think of what a precious
privilege it is to be alive—to breathe, to think, to enjoy,
to love—then make that day count!"*
— *Steve Maraboli, Life, the Truth, and Being Free*

Your body is a miracle. Think about it. In only 9
months, one cell divided 50 times and created YOU. All
of your skin, hair, bones, organs, blood, arms and legs,
everything - in just 9 months.

Throughout the day, take notice of all that your body
does for you and thank it for each action.

Take notice of your motion; walking, sitting,
running, lifting, kneeling. Take notice of your sight,
smell, taste, touch, and what you hear.

Take notice of the very miracle of your breath.

Take notice of the wonder of your blood, and how
the nutrients are being taken throughout your body
with no conscious thought or instructions from you.

Louanne and I have a friend who is a true inspiration. She was born with Spina Bifida and since the age of just a few hours old, she has had over 80 surgeries.

She's an expert on getting around with her wheelchair - and while she could complain and allow thoughts of everything she can't physically do control her life - she instead chooses gratitude, knowing her body is a miracle.

Add reps to your workout by being aware of what your body is saying when you laugh - how does it feel? When you cry? When you're angry? In spite of the labels of those emotions - good or bad -your body is performing miraculous duties, on cue from you.

We have a lot to be grateful for, from our head to our toes!

Day 2
TAKE TIME TO NOTICE

Take notice of all that your body does for you and thank it for that action.

Take notice of your motion - walking, sitting, running, lifting, kneeling.

Take notice of your sight, smell, taste, touch, and what you hear.

Take notice of the very miracle of your BREATH.

DAY 3:
WHEREVER YOU GO

This exercise will work out and sharpen your listening skills.

"'Listening' - The simple act of leaving the land of ME and going fully into the land of YOU without bringing any of ME into the conversation." — Unknown

We've all done it: been in a conversation with someone without really listening to them.

Why? Here are some possible reasons:

- You're busy - thinking of the next thing on your calendar
- Maybe you disagree and dismiss what they're saying
- You could be having other thoughts that have nothing to do with the person in front of you
- Or it might be out of FEAR: if they don't agree with you or are not on the same page, does that somehow make you wrong?

True listening is an act of gratitude. It's recognizing a person for simply being.

Being a good listener is an amazing gift - and validates the person with whom you're talking.

Today, let others share and feel heard first before you speak or share. Let them ask you for advice or input without you offering it because you think they need it.

Make eye contact with them so they know you are fully engaged. Put down your phone, turn off the tv or mute it, invite them to sit down and create an open and welcoming atmosphere for them to speak without feeling like they need to corner you before you run off somewhere.

If the time is truly not right, let them know that and tell them you want to schedule the time because you really want to listen.

Remember when you're listening, it's not about the listener. Sometimes people just need to talk to someone to get something off their chest, or they might need your perspective and respect your input; and most of the time, people just need to be heard, and that's all.

Day 3
WHEREVER YOU GO

Practice good listening.

1. Let other's share first.   How did it feel?

2. Make eye contact.   What did you notice?

3. Create a welcoming atmosphere to share.   How did the person respond?

Being a good listener is an amazing gift.

DAY 4:
SAY THANK YOU

This exercise will transform a compulsive response
into a heartfelt connection.

"If the only prayer you said was thank you,
that would be enough." — *Meister Eckhart*

How many times do you say thank you in a day? Not as
a quick, programmed response - but a real, *genuine*
thank you?

Today's exercise is to write a thank you note to a
person who has had a profound impact on you.

We all interact daily with many people, and just one
action can profoundly impact us. As you think about
the numbers of people you know, you may find the
person you pick might not be from your inner circle of
family and friends.

But to jog your memory and get you thinking of
whom you'd want to write, think of extended family
members, a teacher, boss, co-worker, long distance or
long ago friend, doctor, lawyer, housekeeper, vet, etc?

Be specific in your thank you note telling them what you're thanking them for and why.

Mail it, share it in person, read it to them over the phone. Or, post it on their social media or message them privately.

Think of how they will feel knowing the difference they've made in your life. Feels good doesn't it?

This exercise is so beneficial we recommend writing a thank you note like this **once a week**. Include yourself, your inner circle of family and friends, your spouse, people who provide a service for you like a housekeeper, or your yard service people. You could even write a thank you note to your pet!

This expression of gratitude connects the giver and receiver in a very special way - with amazing blessings for both.

Day 4
SAY THANK YOU

Write a thank you note to someone who has had a profound impact on you - and tell them what it is and why you're thanking them.

Mail it, share it in person, read it to them over the phone, post it on their social media pages or message them privately.

DAY 5:
FIND IT

Today's exercise is a two-fold practice on
mindfulness and being open to new experiences.

"Walk as if you are kissing the Earth with your feet."
— Thích Nhất Hạnh, Peace Is Every Step:
The Path of Mindfulness in Everyday Life

When we do the same things repeatedly, we think we're comfortable - at first. After a while, it gets stagnant, boring. Feeling bored is the opposite of grateful! The solution is to intentionally add in new elements to your life, telling the Universe, "I want to experience more!"

With so much available all the time, why do we tend to revisit the same places, boxing ourselves into this little piece of a very big sky?

Today's exercise is to venture out! Find a new place to walk, bike, run, or mindfully meditate. In this huge world, where have you said, "I want to go *there*," but haven't?

Do that today, even for 15-30 minutes to experience what it's like. As you're walking, biking or running -

what are you experiencing? If you're meditating, are you mindfully aware of your surroundings? Today's quote fits perfectly in this gratitude workout "walk as if you are kissing the earth with your feet." That's a gratitude connection with nature!

What you find today just might be your favorite new place, and that's something to be grateful for!

Day 5
FIND IT

VENTURE OUT!

Find a new place to walk, run, ride your bike, or
meditate. Really take time to notice nature. Write your
reflections in this space.

What did you notice that you haven't noticed before?

DAY 6:
SHOW GRATITUDE

This exercise tracks your Gratitude progress.

*"The miracle of gratitude is that is shifts your perception
to such an extent that it changes the world
you see." — Dr. Robert Holden*

Physical workouts take repetition and daily commitment. If we want to strengthen a muscle, say our arms, we start by lifting a weight we can manage and do a series of repetitions until our arms gets stronger, then we add more weight and repeat the process.

What happens if we stop doing our daily arm workouts? It might take as little as one week's time for us to need to drop down in the weights and start with a lighter set we can manage as we start lifting again.

Gratitude also takes a daily commitment, and that commitment pays off a little bit differently. When we workout our gratitude muscle, we build up a level. And what we've found is something amazing. Our gratitude muscle doesn't lose its strength! You don't need to start back at square one to get back into the gratitude game!

Once you've discovered the power of Gratitude, you actually *can't go backwards*. Sure, there may be days when you feel less grateful, and situations or relationships that really challenge you to exercise gratitude. But amazingly, you won't forget how to be grateful. And, you may find yourself realizing in the midst of that challenging relationship that gratitude is the answer to your problem.

Now, if you really want to see this for yourself, follow today's exercise. Create a Gratitude Journal and track these amazing changes daily!

You can use any small notebook or make one using scraps of paper. Get creative! Decorate the front with stickers or drawings.

Then, every evening, write down one thing you're grateful for in each of the following categories:

Family
Relationships
Your Home Life
Your Work Life
Yourself

If you ARE in the midst of a challenging situation or relationship, start with that category. What's one thing you're grateful for about it? Include yourself daily, it's important to recognize and appreciate who YOU are as well.

Continue writing down one thing you're grateful for in the five areas above for the remaining days in this workout.

When you repeat The 28 Day Gratitude Workout, make a journal for yourself and someone else!

Day 6
SHOW GRATITUDE

Create your own Gratitude Journal. Every evening, write 1 thing you are grateful for from each of the following areas:

1. FAMILY:

2. RELATIONSHIPS:

3. YOUR HOME LIFE:

4. YOUR WORK LIFE:

5. YOURSELF:

DAY 7:
BEING GRATEFUL

This exercise is designed to pull your week together, take a Gratitude self check, and realign yourself before starting week two.

"Piglet noticed that even though he had a Very Small Heart, it could hold a rather large amount of Gratitude."
— *A.A. Milne, Winnie-the-Pooh*

Day 7, congratulations! What have you noticed so far?

Are you more aware of the good?

Did you find yourself paying attention to other people's amazing qualities?

Do you find a sense of peace and joy building as you go about your day?

Gratitude works wonders when we intentionally exercise it.

Over the past 6 days we've given you specific exercises. Today, take the time to write down 7 things you were grateful for over this week, things you may or may not have experienced within the exercises.

They might be related to people, work, family, love, pets, your home, how you feel, your health, your emotional health, or even your ability to be grateful.

Once you have these 7 things noted, write 3 reasons why you're grateful for each.

For example, if one of the things you're grateful for is taking the time to listen to a friend, let's call him Joe, you would say:

"I'm grateful for having the chance to really listen to Joe earlier this week

1) because I didn't realize what he was going through and he really needed to share it and
2) because he had the chance to talk to someone about it and get a different perspective and
3) because I found out he knows a doctor I can refer Jason to for help with his mother's illness."

This exercise will help you really connect in a deeper way with your gratitude as you magnify and strengthen it.

This exercise is so powerful we recommend you make note and do it again on day 14, day 21 and day 28.

Day 7
BEING GRATEFUL

Write down 7 things you are grateful, and 3 reasons you are grateful for each.

1. I am grateful for _____
   Because —
   Because —
   Because —

2.

3.

4.

5.

6.

7.

DAY 8:
MAKE SOMEONES DAY

This exercise helps strengthen the bond
between generosity and gratitude.

*"Feeling gratitude and not expressing it
is like wrapping a present and not giving it."*
— *William Arthur Ward*

We know the phrase, "It's better to give than to receive." But sometimes that doesn't feel true!

Why?

Because giving and generosity are not necessarily the same thing. _Intention_ defines generosity. If I'm just giving something because I "should," or because I've been told to, or because I feel like people expect me to, that's not being generous. The energy behind it is restrictive and leads 'the giver' to feeling a bit less than grateful for being able to give.

When my intention is purely about giving to enhance another person's life, or benefit a situation in a way that is good and right, my intention is naturally tied to gratitude.

Think about it. Think of two different times that you've given. The first situation was compulsory, you gave something but gave it reluctantly or for any of the reasons we've just said. How does that feel?

Now think of a time you gave because you truly wanted to help. Do you feel that? It feels good, it feels open, warm and expansive. That's generosity. It's power packed with intensely good energy, and it's a double whammy, it impacts you and the person or situation you're helping!

Today's exercise is fun and is a double whammy. At some point today, whether you're walking or out somewhere, intentionally drop a coin or two on the ground for someone to find, leave a coin in a vending machine or newstand.

Have you ever found a coin somewhere out of the blue? Kind of cool, right? It's a nice surprise to find a coin on the ground and it makes you feel like you've just won something. You feel lucky, and in that open space, you invite more good into your life. You can help someone invite more good into their life today, just by dropping a coin or two.

Day 8
MAKE SOMEONE'S DAY

Drop a few coins on the ground for someone to find. Share your experience in the space below - how did it feel?

Or leave a few coins in a vending machine, newspaper stand, in a mailbox, office drawer, counter top, jacket pocket or common area for someone to find.

DAY 9:
TAKE TIME TO NOTICE

Today's exercise is a three-fold workout:
physical, spiritual, and mental.

"Gratitude is the ability to experience life as a gift.
It liberates us from the prison of self-preoccupation."
— *John Ortberg, When the Game Is Over,*
It All Goes Back in the Box

Exercise is a great way to show your body how grateful you are for it. Whether you can run, walk, hike, bike, fish, do chair calisthenics or in some other way exercise your body to the best of your ability, you have the opportunity to tell it 'thank you.'

Be aware of the temptation to be a prisoner like today's quote, "Gratitude is the ability to experience life as a gift. It liberates us from the 'prison of self-preoccupation.'" What is that?

We can literally become prisoners to our thoughts even as we're out exercising. Or, for those who don't want to 'think,' listening to music or even talking on the phone during exercise is becoming quite common.

Just for today, we want to exercise without any of the distractions of our thoughts, music, or having a conversation.

While you're working out, take notice of 5 things in nature you're grateful for. For example, the sun on your face, the sounds of the birds, breeze on your skin, the smell of flowers as you pass by.

To be aware of your environment while your are aware of your body is an amazing experience, a complete immersion into being in the 'now' moment.

It's the mindset of the gratitude workout, and that's where we want to be!

Day 9
TAKE TIME TO NOTICE

Take notice of 5 things in nature that you are grateful for as you exercise today.

1.

2.

3.

4.

5.

DAY 10:
WHEREVER YOU GO

Today's exercise is designed to help teach
you both how powerful Gratitude is,
and how powerful you are when you use it!

*"When you focus on gratitude, positive things flow
in more readily, making you even more grateful."*
— Lissa Rankin, *Mind Over Medicine:
Scientific Proof That You Can Heal Yourself*

Today's workout can be both simple and can be extremely hard.

It's repetitive, and it's a way to train yourself with two very powerful and positive words.

Your exercise is to say, "Thank you, thank you" to yourself over and over again throughout the day.

Simple enough? Sure! But take time to really mean it. Just as you take time to truly thank someone else, notice your good, and say thank you.

For some people, this might be hard because many cultures teach that self recognition is a 'bad thing' - it gets labelled as arrogance, conceit, ego.

These same cultures teach us that it's ok, even expected for us to doubt ourselves, question our abilities, beat ourselves up, stress out, and all that results in aching backs, sore necks, tight shoulders, migraines, ulcers, or worse.

Just as every good parent wants to encourage their child and thank them when they do something kind, nice or good, today's exercise is about being gentle with and encouraging to YOURSELF.

It may feel awkward at first, that's ok. Keep doing it. Notice how this makes you feel when you say — and truly mean - thank you, to yourself.

Day 10
WHEREVER YOU GO

Say "thank you, thank you" to yourself through-out the day today.

1. Thank you, thank you for…

2. Thank you, thank you for…

3. Thank you, thank you for…

Take the time to really mean it.

DAY 11:
SAY THANK YOU

This exercise will connect the past to the present.

"Though they only take a second to say, thank you's leave a warm feeling behind that can last for hours."
— Kent Allan Rees, Molly Withers and the Golden Tree

Louanne saw an infographic last year that drew the conclusion that we meet about 80,000 people in an average lifetime. That's based on:

1) an average lifespan of 78.3 years
2) that from age 5 and older we remember people we meet, and
3) that we interact with 3 new people each day!

Of course, that would be different depending upon the country, average lifespan of the people in that country, and whether you live in rural or urban setting - but still, think about it - that's a lot of people!

With that in mind, you could do today's exercise EVERY day and still not finish in your lifetime - WOW!

There are as many ways to say thank you as there are people who've come into our lives. Today's exercise is to think of someone you are very grateful to and for, but you haven't spoken with them in a long time.

Call them! No emails or text. This exercise is meant to connect you, at least by voice, and let them know how grateful you are for them, and why. And it's a great way to get back in touch with them!

That just feels good thinking about it!

Day 11
SAY THANK YOU

Think of someone you are grateful for - but haven't spoken with in a long time. Who is it? Why are you grateful for them?

Surprise them with a phone call - and tell them how grateful you are and why.

DAY 12:
FIND IT

Today's workout will not only help you appreciate all that you have and have had, it will also make you eager for the new things coming!

"Make a pact with yourself today to not be defined by your past. Sometimes the greatest thing to come out of all your hard work isn't what you get for it, but what you become for it. Shake things up today! Be You...Be Free...Share."

— *Steve Maraboli, Life, the Truth, and Being Free*

We could subtitle today's exercise: get up, get out, get grateful!

Sometimes the best way to feel gratitude is to find out what's stopping you. It might be that your same old routine is just keeping you in a box of old habits, and you could easily and quickly get out of that box!

So like today's quote says, make a pact with yourself that you will not be defined by your past - shake things up!

Today's workout is to find a new place to eat a meal. Try keeping it local and healthy, and if you like it, tell your friends about it. Share it on your social media site with the name of the place and how grateful you were for the food, the service, the chef, etc.

There are quite possibly thousands of people in your region, all with incredible culinary skills and talents - and this exercise will connect you with them, help them express their abilities while you can be grateful for a new experience and a meal!

Day 12
FIND IT

VENTURE OUT!

Find a new place to eat a healthy meal and tell your friends and social media networks about it!

What did you like about the food? The atmosphere? The chef? The location? The menu?

DAY 13:
SHOW GRATITUDE

*Today's exercise will serve you year-round, and what
you put into it, is what you get out of it!*

*"Cultivate the habit of being grateful for every good thing
that comes to you, and to give thanks continuously. And
because all things have contributed to your advancement,
you should include all things in your gratitude."*
— *Ralph Waldo Emerson*

A few years ago, Louanne and I started keeping a
gratitude jar. We made a commitment to write down
every thing we were grateful for that happened to us
each day on small pieces of paper. Each item gets its
own piece of paper, then we drop those into a gratitude
jar.

We initially thought, "what a great idea, this will be
a fun!" And it has been.

But we didn't realize that we'd get an extra bonus
when we pulled out each slip of paper, as we
experienced a rush of memories of each good thing,
some we'd even forgotten about! Each memory brought
back a flood of gratitude and an incredible awareness
and joy for life!

For today's exercise, make a gratitude jar for yourself. Make a commitment to add to your gratitude jar every day - at least one thing you were grateful for. Fold it and put that paper into the jar.

When the jar is full (or if you find a day you're feeling less than grateful) take all the pieces of paper in the jar and read them, experience them. Your day will completely change, guaranteed!

Then start over! This is an amazing exercise when done individually, and incredibly powerful for couples or friends, so share this exercise with one other person!

If you're repeating this 28 day workout, make a gratitude jar for someone else. This is definitely an exercise where what you put in, is what you take out!

Day 13
SHOW GRATITUDE

Make yourself a Gratitude Jar. Add at least one thing you're grateful for daily. You can select anything throughout the day or use the list below to prompt you.

1. FAMILY:

2. RELATIONSHIPS:

3. YOUR HOME LIFE:

4. YOUR WORK LIFE:

5. YOURSELF:

DAY 14:
BEING GRATEFUL

This exercise will help you develop or re-connect
to an appreciation of what you have.

"Do not spoil what you have by desiring what you have not;
remember that what you now have was once among
the things you only hoped for."
— *Epicurus*

Do you remember how you felt when you got your first
bike? Your first car? Or maybe your first wheelchair?
What did it look like? How fast was it? Did it have any
special features?

That memory probably made you smile, for any
number of reasons. And maybe the most important
one is because you remember how it felt just knowing
you had a new mode of transportation.

But how quickly that can turn into routine, and we
start wanting a newer version, a faster version, a bigger
version.

Today's exercise is to become aware of and have a
renewed appreciation for your mode of transportation.
What do you use to get around from place to place?

It might be your car, bike, truck, train, motorcycle, maybe it's the bus, a taxi, your wheelchair - or even yes - your legs!

We forget to thank and be grateful for the very things that others may not have. It may not be the newest, it might even have some cosmetic or mechanical issues. But focusing on what it does NOT have, is the opposite of gratitude and closes us off from our good.

When was the last time you cleaned your car inside and out? Washed your bike? Treated your legs to a massage? Do one thing today to take care of your mode of transportation, and as you're using it, say thank you.

List three things about your car, or bike, or wheelchair or legs that you do appreciate. As Epicurus so wisely taught long ago, "Do not spoil what you have by desiring what you have not; remember that what you now have was once among the things you only hoped for"!

Day 14
BEING GRATEFUL

Be aware of and appreciate your current mode of transportation.

Do one thing today to take care of it - clean it, wash it, fill the tires, change the oil. As you do it, say 'Thank you.' Write down 3 things you are grateful for about it:

1.

2.

3.

DAY 15:
MAKE SOMEONE'S DAY

This exercise will help strengthen your heart muscle.

"The unthankful heart discovers no mercies; but the thankful heart will find, in every hour, some heavenly blessings."

— *Henry Ward Beecher*

Today's exercise is about taking action. How many times during the day do you cross paths with people? In the elevator, on the stairs, going in and out of doors, on a bus, in a mall, at a store?

Do you interact, or simply pay them no attention? The fact that you are on the same elevator, or standing in the same line, or shopping in the same aisle of your grocery store may mean something more than coincidence.

The first insight of the Celestine Prophecy, a popular book about spirituality, talks specifically about this. Here's a quote from the book:

"I don't think that anything happens by coincidence. No one is here by accident. Everyone who crosses our

path has a message for us. Otherwise, they would have taken another path, or left earlier or later. The fact that these people are here means that they are in our lives for some reason."

Doesn't it make you kind of curious to know the reason?!

Today, step out of your comfort zone. All day today, when you see people choose to either smile at them, wave, say hello or wish them a good day.

Take notice of how good it feels to take action, and know it probably also makes them feel good.

This exercise strengthens your heart muscle and you just might meet someone 'coincidentally on purpose.'

Day 15
MAKE SOMEONE'S DAY

Take notice of everyone you meet today and acknowledge them - with a smile, a wave or by saying hello.

Share your experience in the space below - how did it feel?

...how did they respond?

DAY 16:
TAKE TIME TO NOTICE

Today's workout is an exercise in awareness.

"The experiment he used to discover this included bottles filled with water, that were set under either a positive or a negative influence. For example, some bottles of water were wrapped with written notes, with the writing facing inside the bottle that said, "thank you." This was done in various languages. No matter what language was used, the water in these bottles, when frozen, created complete crystals that were lovely to behold." - from Dr. Masaru Emoto's website, www.masaru-emoto.net.

In 1999, Dr. Masaru Emoto published "Messages from Water" a revolutionary study on the power of words, thoughts, music, and vibrations in the formation of water crystals. Dr. Emoto studied water and the impacts of negative or positive vibrations for more than 20 years, and his discoveries have been translated to over 35 languages.

When he wrapped the bottles of water in the words 'love and gratitude,' the crystals were exceptionally well formed and beautiful.

Knowing that our bodies are about 70% water, and that water is a major part of our everyday lives, should motivate us to be intentionally grateful as we interact with it.

Today's exercise is to take notice of water throughout the day; when you drink it, take a shower, bathe, wash your hands.

Be grateful that you have a clean, fresh unlimited water supply which is not true in many parts of our world. Remember Dr. Emoto's study and every time you use water today, say thank you.

This exercise will impact your skin, digestion and overall health as well as making you more aware of water, to appreciate and conserve it and to drink more for the benefit of your body.

Day 16
TAKE TIME TO NOTICE

Take notice of water throughout the day - drinking, bathing, or washing your hands.

List 5 ways you are grateful for water.

1.

2.

3.

4.

5.

DAY 17:
WHEREVER YOU GO

Practicing this exercise will help you de-stress your life!

"Breath is the finest gift of nature.
Be grateful for this wonderful gift."
— *Amit Ray, Beautify your Breath - Beautify your Life*

It's something we don't have to consciously do, but perhaps we should be more aware of it. Or at least take time to be intentional about it several times a day. What is it? Breathing.

Stress causes a great deal of irregularity in breathing. Some people become so stressed they hyperventilate. Others tend to breathe in shallow gasps, or may stop breathing when anxious such as the phrase "I held my breath."

Breathing is essential to life, and why in today's quote, Amit Ray calls it "the finest gift of nature." We also talk about it in phrases to define aspects of life: "In the same breath" - meaning two sides stated at once. "Take a breath" - and calm down. "She's a breath of fresh air" - a welcome change. "Save your breath" - don't waste your time. And "As long as I have a breath left in me" - I'm stating a serious commitment.

Today's exercise is to help you notice your breathing, all day. Think of how your breathing was upon waking, be aware of it in the shower, as you work out, as you drive or sit at your desk or in front of your computer.

Several times today practice taking a deep breath in, and as you inhale say to yourself "I am feeling grateful".

Be aware of the breath filling your nostrils, filling your lungs.

As you exhale, say to yourself "Thank You."

This exercise has so many benefits - do it several times every day!

Day 17
WHEREVER YOU GO

Be aware of your breathing.

Several times today practice breathing:

1. As you inhale, think: "I am feeling grateful." How did that feel?

2. As you exhale, think: "Thank you." How did that feel?

What do you notice about yourself?

DAY 18:
SAY THANK YOU

This exercise will add zest to your friendship!

"We must find time to stop and thank the people who make a difference in our lives." — *John F. Kennedy*

While we often thank people for gifts or actions of the present, today we're reaching out to thank them for no reason at all.

Today's exercise is to contact someone you are very grateful for and ask them to meet for coffee or a meal. Your gratitude is about them, for just being themselves, for being in your life.

The main reason for meeting them is to tell them face to face how grateful you are for them, and why. When you set up the meeting, just invite them out and then at the meeting, make it about them. Use the time to find out how they really are.

Give them the gift of your listening to them, asking heartfelt questions and really connecting with them. Often our get togethers include talking about day to day tasks or work happenings. Not this time. This time is about you connecting with this one other person heart to heart.

If they invite you to their home, take something with you - flowers, a card, a small gift.

Plan on paying for the meal and surprise them. You can even excuse yourself and let the waiter know you will be taking care of the bill before it's brought to your table.

Think of any other details, little touches that would add to the experience you're giving your friend. Do they like flowers? Call ahead and have a special arrangement as a centerpiece on your table. Does the restaurant staff sing to customers for their birthdays? Ask if they will sing a special rendition, using "We're Grateful for You" instead of "Happy Birthday to You" for your friend.

Make this time a special time for no reason other than to express gratitude for who they are and all they mean to you.

This exercise is good for your spirit and soul, and will certainly raise their spirit as well.

Day 18
SAY THANK YOU

Invite a friend you are grateful for to join you for a meal. Plan to pay for their meal. Make this time all about them, and tell them why you are grateful for them. **Write who you invited and why, and describe what the experience was like.**

DAY 19:
FIND IT

This exercise is great for your health, heart and happiness!

"Acknowledging the good that you already have in your life is the foundation for all abundance."
— *Eckhart Tolle, A New Earth: Awakening to Your Life's Purpose*

Do you own a computer, laptop, or smart phone? Who made it? I don't mean the company, I mean the person or persons who crafted the material, made the motherboard, soldered the circuits together?

Are you reading a book? Who wrote it? Who helped build the printing press that printed it? Who made the ink that went into the press?

Today's exercise is about finding out who is responsible for the things that occur in our day to day world, and if you can't find out, to at least be *intentionally aware* of them.

Think of your workplace - do you have a cleaning team? A yard service company? If you have the opportunity to see them in action, say thank you in person. But if you can't say thank you in person, take a moment to acknowledge all they do, and say thank you for this person, to yourself.

It might be a neighbor, someone at work, an employee at your favorite restaurant, your gym, or at the post office.

It could be a hairdresser or someone in a service industry that helps you where you live or work, the sanitation team who empties your garbage and picks up your recycling, the electric company employees who make electricity possible in your home, or the water department employees who help provide water to your home or office. Or it might be the person who helped build your car, or your coffee maker, or refrigerator.

Everything we have came from the skills and talents of other people. Our things are not just things - they are the creations of other human beings, who in turn own things created by other people.

As you use the items in your home or office, as you get dressed or take out the garbage, as you drive to or from the store, say thanks to those responsible.

The message will be felt! And it's a great exercise for good health, a healthy heart, and happiness!

Day 19
FIND IT

ACT INTENTIONALLY!

Find out who is responsible for the daily
items you use and event that occur in your life.

Thank them in person, or thank them in thought.

DAY 20:
SHOW GRATITUDE

Today's workout will connect you, your memories and nature for years to come!

"Plant the seeds of gratitude to grow and enjoy the abundance of life."
— *Debasish Mridha*

A few years ago, Louanne and I took a multi-week road trip around the United States, visiting our friends spread out over 5,000 miles. We asked our friends and anyone we met along the way - two questions: what does gratitude mean to you, and what are you grateful for?

Our trip, *Gratitude Across America*, turned into a 40 minute video we treasure, and posted on our YouTube channel. (www.youtube.com/watchmvvptv) We loved discovering the many ways our friends, family and even strangers expressed gratitude. The whole trip was like getting shots of gratitude every day!

One of our friends expressed gratitude in a very special way - a way that connected her with nature and with her friends multiple times a day. And, it's today's workout:

Plant a gratitude tree, get a potted plant, or take a snippet of a plant in your home or backyard and replant it - as a representation of your gratitude.

It might represent a particular person or several friendships. It might represent a stage in your life or a very specific item, thing, lesson you are grateful for.

The purpose of this exercise is that every time you see it, it's beauty, how it's growing, it will remind you of your gratitude. You'll feel grateful and you'll remember the who or what behind why you planted it.

When you repeat this 28 day workout, buy a tree or potted plant for someone else and let them know it's a gratitude tree or gratitude plant.

If you have the space, start a "Gratitude Garden," with each member of the garden representing a unique thing or person you're grateful for.

Now that's the way to connect, your memories and nature for years to come!

Day 20
SHOW GRATITUDE

Plant a Gratitude Tree, Gratitude Plant or take a cutting from a plant in your home or garden.

Who or what does it represent?

What will you think of when you see it?

DAY 21:
BEING GRATEFUL

This exercise will strengthen your ability to taste!

"The grateful heart sits at a continuous feast."
— Anonymous

Many of us were raised to give thanks before a meal, and many more of us have felt the relief that comes from being able to eat something when we're hungry. This is truly a gift, and one that millions of people do not get to experience on a daily basis.

Hunger Statistics from the World Food Programme stated that in 2015 approximately "795 million people in the world do not have enough food to lead a healthy active life."

To put it another way, that's 1 in 9 people on earth.

Today's exercise is to be grateful for everything you eat and drink today. Yes, it includes saying thank you for the food you have, but we're taking it a few steps further. In honor of your body, try to keep it healthy, being thankful that the food you're eating will nourish your body with nutrients and vitamins it needs to perform the functions you ask it to.

With every thing you put in your mouth, take a moment to experience it's texture, taste, temperature. Think of how well you're enjoying it as you eat or drink. Then take a moment to think of all the people it took to get this food ... to you.

As an example, here's what it would look like doing this exercise with a piece of fruit - let's say an apple. Think of all the people who put energy into making that apple available to you. Who put it out for you to purchase at the market? Who sold it or distributed it to that market? Who farmed it? Who planted the seed and nurtured the tree it grew on? As you enjoy your next apple, say thank you to everyone who made it possible for you to eat the apple that is nourishing your body.

Take a moment to thank all of the people that were involved in everything you eat or drink today. Get into the habit of doing this every day - it's good for your body and soul, and will make your food taste so much better!

Day 21
BEING GRATEFUL

Be aware of your food and drink, how it tastes.

Be aware of all the people who made that food or drink possible for you. Write down the steps it took to get the food or drink to you, and 3 things you are grateful for about it.

1.

2.

3.

DAY 22:
MAKE SOMEONE'S DAY

This exercise will turn you into a masterful painter, creating magnificent scenes in your life and the lives of other people.

"One grateful thought is a ray of sunshine.
A hundred such thoughts paint a sunrise.
A thousand will rival the glaring sky at noonday -
for gratitude is light against the darkness."
— *Richelle E. Goodrich, Smile Anyway:*
Quotes, Verse, & Grumblings for Every Day of the Year

This quote really speaks to the power of Gratitude!

Today's exercise will brighten your sky as well as countless others! It's easy to do, and can be repeated everywhere.

The exercise is simple, and powerful:

Using sticky notes, write kind, empowering words and thoughts on them, then leave the sticky notes on mirrors, doors, in elevators, anywhere you go today - placing them where people will notice. Keep each note short but purposeful. Here are a few examples:

You can do it!   I feel good!   You are amazing!
Laugh all day!   Smile!   Thank you!
I did it!   You inspire me!   I inspire people!

And on and on. Be creative with what you say as well as where you leave each note.

Keep some around for yourself as a reminder, using your favorite affirmations. Stay positive and empowering.

Imagine someone walking into an elevator and seeing a sticky note on the elevator door as the door closes. I see them smiling, don't you? Or sitting down at their computer to see a sticky note on their screen with a few words of encouragement. Or arriving at their car after leaving the office to find, "You inspire people!" on the driver's side window to greet them.

The opportunities are endless with this exercise, as is the joy and gratitude you - and they - will feel.

And it's a good exercise for your mind in thinking of positive, empowering words and phrases, and great for your memory to hold onto for when you, or someone else, might need them.

Day 22
MAKE SOMEONE'S DAY

Write kind, empowering messages on sticky notes and leave them for people to find. Use the space below to share your experiences. How did you feel? What did you write on the notes?

1.

2.

3.

Remember to leave a few notes for yourself!

DAY 23:
TAKE TIME TO NOTICE

Today's workout will strengthen your
awareness and de-clutter your life!

*"Be thankful for what you have; you'll end up having more.
If you concentrate on what you don't have,
you will never, ever have enough."*
-- Oprah Winfrey

Can you answer these questions off the top of your
head?

How many shirts do you own?
How many pants? Jeans? Jackets? Pairs of shoes?

Chances are, you have no idea. But there may be days
when you stand in front of your closet thinking or
saying out loud, "I have nothing to wear."

To put this into perspective - in an article by David
Bernstein in the New York Times, people in India may
have only one or two items of clothing. But millions of
people in the West are also in need of clothing. If you're
one of the those who don't, that's reason enough to be
grateful.

Today's step by step exercise is to take a good look at your closet.

Step 1:
Notice all the array of clothing and shoes you have to choose from when you're getting dressed today. Appreciate the many combinations of outfits you can create by taking one shirt to multiple pants or jeans or skirts. Instead of looking at your closet and thinking of what you "don't have" - see all that you do.

Step 2:
Write down the categories: shirts, pants, jeans, capri's, skirts, sweaters, shoes, boots, sandals. Then physically count the numbers of each category that you currently have hanging in your closet. Then do the same with the drawers in your dresser or chest.

Step 3:
Today or sometime this week, go through all of your clothes and shoes and set aside anything you no longer choose to wear. How many bags did you fill? Find a person or organization that will put those items to wonderful use!

Not only are you de-cluttering your closet, which is a healthy and feel good move, you are also helping someone else who truly may not have anything to wear!

When you repeat this 28 day course, do this exercise with another closet or drawer, or with another type of item, such as your books, CD's or DVD's, making sure you follow this three step process to feel the gratitude of all you have.

Day 23
TAKE TIME TO NOTICE

STEP 1: Take notice of all the variety of clothing and shoes you own!

STEP 2: Write down the categories and count them. (Shirts, Pants, Skirts, Polos, Dresses, Suits)

STEP 3: Set aside any items you no longer want and give them to someone or an organization who does.

How many bags did you collect?

DAY 24:
WHEREVER YOU GO

This exercise will connect your heart and your mind.

*"Open your eyes and see how many gifts there are to
unwrap. Notice the presence of your presents.
It's not your life that is disappointing: it's your mind."*
— *Gregg Krech, Naikan: Gratitude, Grace,
and the Japanese Art of Self-Reflection*

You've probably heard the saying, "Walk the talk"
meaning, actually DO what you say you will do, live the
life you talk about.

Today's exercise can be called "Walk the Gratitude
Talk" - and to expand it just a little, we can call it "Walk
or ROLL the Gratitude Talk".

Wherever you go, walking, driving, biking,
running, at home, in the office, wherever you are -
notice the thoughts and feelings you're thinking and
feeling.

This is Day 24, and you've experienced 23 days of
exercises that have prepared you for this exercise. It
means being present in your own presence. Being
aware of what you're thinking and feeling - which isn't
always easy to do.

Have you ever been lost in thought, only to realize minutes - maybe hours later - that you've been consumed with your own thoughts or have created some fantasy stories about a situation you're dealing with? These stories will never happen, and most often they're negative in nature, but you're pulled into them, and they may go on and on and on!

People who practice meditation call this the monkey mind - your mind is off and running and you're fully participating in thoughts and creating stories without even realizing it.

Have you ever been around someone who keeps rehashing something negative? Did you feel the negativity flowing from them? It's toxic and we most often don't like being around people in the midst of that toxicity.

So how do you practice walking (or rolling) the gratitude talk? It starts with taking a mental checkup. Set your alarm to ring on the hour, every hour. When the alarm goes off, ask yourself, what am I thinking and feeling? You will probably catch yourself at some time or several times 'lost in thought' or creating little stories.

What are the stories or thoughts about? How do they make you feel? If they're negative and don't feel so good, change them.

The Gratitude Walk Roll is about positive, happy, helpful words, thoughts and actions. It's inspired from your heart. Taking a mental checkup will allow your heart to re-align your mind. For example:

Negative thoughts about a friend can be shifted by *listing five strengths you admire, respect, or like about that person.* It doesn't mean you're ignoring the situation. Instead, you're changing your thought pattern, taking control of your thoughts, you are CHOOSING how you will respond instead of letting your monkey mind swing you around. And that feels so much better!

Keep setting your alarm for these mental checkups until you find yourself doing them spontaneously. And when you do it spontaneously, say Thank You to your heart, for pulling you back into a space of gratitude which is so much better for your health and well being.

Day 24
WHEREVER YOU GO

Walk or ROLL the Gratitude Talk.

1. Notice your thoughts and feelings throughout the day. What are you thinking? Feeling?

2. Take a mental check-up every hour. What's on your mind?

3. Do you catch yourself telling stories to yourself?

The more you practice this exercise, the more aware you are of your own thoughts.

DAY 25:
SAY THANK YOU!

Today's workout will flex your creativity muscle!

*"Extending gratitude to another says, "I see what
you've done and I thank you for the energy you put forth."*
— Molly Friedenfeld, The Book of Simple Human Truths

Years ago, Louanne's sister decided she wasn't going to
buy any of her friends presents for their birthdays or
for holiday gifts. Instead, she spent the entire year
making gifts for them. Some gifts were as simple as
hand-crafted cards, other gifts were a bit more
extensive and took days to weeks for her to create.

At the time, Louanne thought of only one thing -
would her friends really want something she made for
them, rather than something store bought and better
quality? But today as she looks around our home, she
realizes the items she cherishes most of all were not
store-bought gifts, but items that family or friends took
time to craft especially for her.

It's not the quality or being hand-made that makes
this difference. It's the thought behind each item that
makes it a cherished treasure.

Today's exercise is to think of someone whom you are grateful for and show them by making something for them. Get creative! Do you remember the last time you exercised your creativity muscle? Kids naturally love to create this way, and as we get older many of us tend to set our creative expression aside.

Here are a few examples:

- Write them a song or a poem
- Draw them a picture
- Create a Gratitude board
- Shoot a short video with your phone of you speaking to them, telling them why you're grateful.

The main objective is to be creative, think of who they are and what makes you grateful. Find ways to represent that gratitude, what would that look like for this person you have chosen?

Creative expression is an important part of many health and wellness programs and is believed to add years and energy to your life - and that's also something to be grateful for!

Day 25
SAY THANK YOU

Make a homemade gift for someone you are grateful for - get creative!

What did you make?

How did you feel creating it?

How did they receive it?

DAY 26:
FIND IT

Today's exercise will strengthen gratitude around the world!

*"When the Altitude of Gratitude grows in Multitude
with Certitude the World will perceive Beatitude"*
— *Musab Faiyazuddin*

Congratulations! You've nearly completed The 28 Day Gratitude Workout! By now you've experienced a variety of exercises, some may have been more challenging than others, and we'd love to hear about them.

Today's exercise is a two step process:

Step 1:
Think back on your last 25 days of gratitude exercises. Think of three lessons that really speak to you.

Why did they speak to you?

What did you learn?

How did they benefit your life?

When we experience good in our lives, we like to share it - so chances are, you've already been talking with your friends about the lessons you've learned and how you've grown. Think now of people you know who could benefit from the lessons you've learned.

Step 2:
Reach out to one to five people and create a Gratitude Workout group that meets or talks once a week to share your experiences and lessons.

Your experience may be just the thing your friend or co-worker needs to hear to change his or her life, add positive thoughts to their life or help them live in a state of gratitude that is both fulfilling and fun!
(Share this exercise on our Facebook page!)

Day 26
FIND IT

Step 1: Think of 3 lessons you've learned from this course. What are they?

Step 2: Create a Gratitude Workout Group with 1-5 other people. Who are they?

DAY 27:
SHOW GRATITUDE!

Today's exercise will strengthen the human bond.

"Gratitude begins in our hearts and then dovetails into behavior. It almost always makes you willing to be of service, which is where the joy resides... When you are aware of all that has been given to you, in your lifetime and the past few days, it is hard not to be humbled, and pleased to give back." — Anne Lamott, Help Thanks Wow: The Three Essential Prayers

You are on a natural course now, a road paved with Gratitude that quickly takes you from need, to thanks, to giving back. And the giving back is incredibly rewarding and creates even more Gratitude! Anne Lamott, author of Help Thanks Wow: The Three Essential Prayers, summarized this beautifully in today's quote:

"Gratitude begins in our hearts and then dovetails into behavior. It almost always makes you willing to be of service, which is where the joy resides."

Today's exercise is to get out into the world, find someone or some organization to be of service to today. It may even be a stranger. Just allow yourself to be open to finding a situation in which your energy, time and talent can be put to good use.

Be open to seeing these opportunities. It might be a mother needing help changing her tire in order to drive her child to school. Or a neighbor just back from the hospital who could really use a home cooked meal. It might be a nonprofit organization in need of volunteers. Or your son's friend at school who could use the jacket your son grew out of.

When you're open to the possibilities, the opportunities to make a difference are endless, and they will make a difference in your life as well.

At the end of the day, take 5 minutes to write about your experiences. What were they? How did they make you feel? How did they impact you, or impact others?

This is a great exercise to do at least once a month - but be careful, it's so good you'll want to do more. You might find yourself being open and available all the time!

Day 27
SHOW GRATITUDE

Be of service today.

Find someone or an organization to be of service to today. It might be a neighbor or a nonprofit organization which needs volunteer help.

This evening, write about your experiences.

Where did you go?

How did you help?

What did it feel like?

DAY 28:
BEING GRATEFUL!

This exercise will strengthen your self-esteem,
and is recommended to continue daily!

*"You simply will not be the same person two months from
now after consciously giving thanks each day for the
abundance that exists in your life."*
— *Sarah Ban Breathnach, Simple Abundance*

Chances are good that over the past 27 days, you've had to stretch outside of your comfort zone just a bit. And, while it might have been scary at first, how do you feel now having stretched? Strengthening our self-esteem is an amazing experience, it is the essence of empowerment. Self confidence feels GOOD, and magnifies the amount of gratitude we can feel!

It's also important to understand the very personal process of gratitude - it happens within YOU. I can't feel your gratitude just as you cannot feel mine. Much like love, gratitude is completely personal. I cannot love your spouse for you, and I cannot be grateful for your spouse - for you. That's something you and only you can do, for you.

So the very fact that you can and have expressed gratitude for the past 27 days means you have tapped into areas in your life and made a conscious decision to recognize them as good and valuable. You've made a conscious decision to be aware of your thoughts and take charge of them. You've made a conscious decision to check in with your feelings and understand them. And you've made a conscious decision to remain open to the possibilities and let Life give you even more goodness.

That's huge, and a lot of work, and now is the time to take notice of the work you've done.

It's perfect for us to end this 28 day workout with a focus on YOU. Today's exercise is to take note of all the things you have to be grateful for about yourself.

Take as much time as you need at the end of the day today, and write down all the things you've discovered about how awesome and incredible it is to be you! Taking pride in your self growth is a good thing to do when you're coming at it from a space of gratitude! It's an expression of love for yourself, and heightens your sense of self worth, builds your self esteem, strengthens your self love and your confidence to do whatever you want to do.

Day 28
BEING GRATEFUL

Take note of all the things you have to be grateful for about YOURSELF.

By feeling true Gratitude for yourself, you strengthen your ability to be Grateful for others!

CONCLUSION

"When you practice gratefulness, there is a sense of respect towards others." - The Dalai Lama

CONGRATULATIONS!

You've completed The 28 Day Gratitude Workout, well done! You are simply not the same person you were when you started this workout - and your exercises in Gratitude will continue to shift you. We recommend doing this workout again and again - you'll find the exercises teach different lessons each time. You can repeat the exercises in order - Day 1 - 28, or try a different approach and focus on each category. We've included a calendar of The 28 Day Gratitude Workout in Appendix A, and the exercises are listed by category in Appendix B. We've also included additional workout sheets for each day in Appendix C.

Louanne and I are developing more courses in the series of The 28 Day Gratitude Workout (TM) and you can keep current with the latest courses by visiting our website: www.the28daygratitudeworkout.com and our Facebook page. Sign up for our email list to receive the most current updates, and share your Stories of

Gratitude with us! Email us at grateful@the28daygratitudeworkout.com.

Thank you, Thank you!

Sharon & Louanne

APPENDIX A - Calendar (use w/Table of Contents)

	MAKE SOMEONE'S DAY	TAKE TIME TO NOTICE	WHEREVER YOU GO	SAY THANK YOU	FIND IT	SHOW GRATITUDE	BEING GRATEFUL
WEEK 1	Compliment yourself & others	Thank your body	Practice true listening	Write a thank you note	Exercise in a new place	Create a Gratitude Journal	List 7 gratitudes from the week, & 3 reasons why for each
WEEK 2	Drop a coin on the ground or leave in a vending machine	Exercise while noticing 5 things you're grateful for in nature	Say "thank you" to yourself all day	Call someone you're grateful for and tell them why	Find a new place to eat a meal and share why you're grateful	Create a Gratitude Jar	Clean or improve your mode of transportation & list gratitudes for it
WEEK 3	Smile, wave, say hello to everyone you meet today	Be grateful for your fresh water supply	Practice gratitude in your breathing	Treat someone to a meal & tell them why you're grateful for them	Find out who's responsible to item you use, thank them	Plant a Gratitude Tree, Plant or Garden	Be grateful for (& mindful of) what you eat and drink today
WEEK 4	Leave sticky notes with empowering message	Take a good look at your closet	Walk & Roll the Gratitude Talk with mental checkups	Make something for someone you're grateful for	List 3 lessons from the past 25 days you're grateful for and why	Be of service to someone or an organization today	List all the things you are thankful for about YOU

APPENDIX B - Categories

MAKE SOMEONE'S DAY
Compliment yourself & others - p.7
Drop a coin on the ground/vending machine - p.29
Smile, wave, say hello to everyone today - p.50
Leave sticky notes with empowering messages - p.71

TAKE TIME TO NOTICE
Thank your body - p.10
Exercise while noticing 5 things you're grateful for in nature - p.32
Be grateful for your fresh water supply - p.53
Take a good look at your closet - p.74

WHEREVER YOU GO
Practice true listening - p.13
Say "thank you" to yourself all day - p.35
Practice gratitude in your breathing - p.56
Walk & Roll the Gratitude Talk - p.78

SAY THANK YOU
Write a thank you note - p.16
Call someone you're grateful for, tell them why - p.38
Treat someone to a meal, tell them why you're grateful for them - p.59
Make something for someone - p.82

FIND IT

Exercise in a new place - p.19

Find a new place to eat a healthy meal, share why you're grateful - p.41

Find out who's responsible for items you use, thank them - p.62

List 3 lessons from the past 25 days you're grateful for & why - p.85

SHOW GRATITUDE

Create a Gratitude Journal - p.22

Create a Gratitude Jar - p.44

Plant a Gratitude Tree - p.65

Be of service to someone / an organization today - p.88

BEING GRATEFUL

List 7 gratitudes from the week, 3 reasons why - p.26

Clean or improve your mode of transport & list gratitudes for it -p.47

Be grateful for (& mindful of) what you eat and drink today - p.68

List all you are thankful for about YOU - p.91

APPENDIX C

Additional pages of worksheets 1-28 for repeat use. Make copies of these for additional workouts as needed.

Day 1
MAKE SOMEONE'S DAY

Give yourself three to five compliments. Write them here and then say them out loud. They might be about a skill you've developed or a talent you have, or something you've accomplished recently, or about your hair or body - the point is to notice, acknowledge and compliment 3-5 things about yourself.

1.

2.

3.

Compliment others throughout the day - your family members, neighbors, co-workers, even strangers.

Day 2
TAKE TIME TO NOTICE

Take notice of all that your body does for you and thank it for that action.

Take notice of your motion - walking, sitting, running, lifting, kneeling.

Take notice of your sight, smell, taste, touch, and what you hear.

Take notice of the very miracle of your BREATH.

Day 3
WHEREVER YOU GO

Practice good listening.

1. Let other's share first. How did it feel?

2. Make eye contact. What did you notice?

3. Create a welcoming atmosphere to share. How did the person respond?

Being a good listener is an amazing gift.

Day 4
SAY THANK YOU

Write a thank you note to someone who has had a profound impact on you - and tell them what it is and why you're thanking them.

Mail it, share it in person, read it to them over the phone, post it on their social media pages or message them privately.

Day 5
FIND IT

Find a new place to walk, run, ride your bike, or meditate. Really take time to notice nature. Write your reflections in this space.

What did you notice that you haven't noticed before?

Day 6
SHOW GRATITUDE

Create your own Gratitude Journal. Every evening, write 1 thing you are grateful for from each of the following areas:

1. FAMILY:

2. RELATIONSHIPS:

3. YOUR HOME LIFE:

4. YOUR WORK LIFE:

5. YOURSELF:

Day 7
BEING GRATEFUL

Write down 7 things you are grateful, and 3 reasons you are grateful for each.

1. I am grateful for _____
   Because —
   Because —
   Because —

2.

3.

4.

5.

6.

7.

Day 8
MAKE SOMEONE'S DAY

Drop a few coins on the ground for someone to find.
Share your experience in the space below - how did it
feel?

Or leave a few coins in a vending machine, newspaper
stand, in a mailbox, office drawer, counter top, jacket
pocket or common area for someone to find.

Day 9
TAKE TIME TO NOTICE

Take notice of 5 things in nature that you are grateful for as you exercise today.

1.

2.

3.

4.

5.

Day 10
WHEREVER YOU GO

Say "thank you, thank you" to yourself through-out the day today.

1. Thank you, thank you for...

2. Thank you, thank you for...

3. Thank you, thank you for...

Take the time to really mean it.

Day 11
SAY THANK YOU

Think of someone you are grateful for - but haven't spoken with in a long time. Who is it? Why are you grateful for them?

Surprise them with a phone call - and tell them how grateful you are and why.

Day 12
FIND IT

VENTURE OUT!

Find a new place to eat a healthy meal and tell your friends and social media networks about it!

What did you like about the food? The atmosphere? The chef? The location? The menu?

Day 13
SHOW GRATITUDE

Make yourself a Gratitude Jar. Add at least one thing you're grateful for daily. You can select anything throughout the day or use the list below to prompt you.

1. FAMILY:

2. RELATIONSHIPS:

3. YOUR HOME LIFE:

4. YOUR WORK LIFE:

5. YOURSELF:

Day 14
BEING GRATEFUL

Be aware of and appreciate your current mode of transportation.

Do one thing today to take care of it - clean it, wash it, fill the tires, change the oil. As you do it, say 'Thank you.' Write down 3 things you are grateful for about it:

1.

2.

3.

Day 15
MAKE SOMEONE'S DAY

Take notice of everyone you meet today and acknowledge them - with a smile, a wave or by saying hello.

Share your experience in the space below - how did it feel?

...how did they respond?

Day 16
TAKE TIME TO NOTICE

Take notice of water throughout the day - drinking, bathing, or washing your hands.

List 5 ways you are grateful for water.

1.

2.

3.

4.

5.

Day 17
WHEREVER YOU GO

Be aware of your breathing.

Several times today practice breathing:

1.   As you inhale, think: "I am feeling grateful." How did that feel?

2.   As you exhale, think: "Thank you." How did that feel?

What do you notice about yourself?

Day 18
SAY THANK YOU

Invite a friend you are grateful for to join you for a meal. Plan to pay for their meal. Make this time all about them, and tell them why you are grateful for them. **Write who you invited and why, and describe what the experience was like.**

Day 19
FIND IT

ACT INTENTIONALLY!

Find out who is responsible for the daily
items you use and event that occur in your life.

Thank them in person, or thank them in thought.

Day 20
SHOW GRATITUDE

Plant a Gratitude Tree, Gratitude Plant or take a cutting from a plant in your home or garden.

Who or what does it represent?

What will you think of when you see it?

Day 21
BEING GRATEFUL

Be aware of your food and drink, how it tastes.

Be aware of all the people who made that food or drink possible for you. Write down the steps it took to get the food or drink to you, and 3 things you are grateful for about it.

1.

2.

3.

Day 22
MAKE SOMEONE'S DAY

Write kind, empowering messages on sticky notes and leave them for people to find. Use the space below to share your experiences. How did you feel? What did you write on the notes?

1.

2.

3.

Remember to leave a few notes for yourself!

Day 23
TAKE TIME TO NOTICE

STEP 1: Take notice of all the variety of clothing and shoes you own!

STEP 2: Write down the categories and count them. (Shirts, Pants, Skirts, Polos, Dresses, Suits)

STEP 3: Set aside any items you no longer want and give them to someone or an organization who does.

How many bags did you collect?

Day 24
WHEREVER YOU GO

Walk or ROLL the Gratitude Talk.

1. Notice your thoughts and feelings throughout the day. What are you thinking? Feeling?

2. Take a mental check-up every hour. What's on your mind?

3. Do you catch yourself telling stories to yourself?

The more you practice this exercise, the more aware you are of your own thoughts.

Day 25
SAY THANK YOU

Make a homemade gift for someone you are grateful for - get creative!

What did you make?

How did you feel creating it?

How did they receive it?

Day 26
FIND IT

Step 1: Think of 3 lessons you've learned from this course. What are they?

Step 2: Create a Gratitude Workout Group with 1-5 other people. Who are they?

Day 27
SHOW GRATITUDE

Be of service today.

Find someone or an organization to be of service to today. It might be a neighbor or a nonprofit organization which needs volunteer help.

This evening, write about your experiences.

Where did you go?

How did you help?

What did it feel like?

Day 28
BEING GRATEFUL

Take note of all the things you have to be grateful for about YOURSELF.

By feeling true Gratitude for yourself, you strengthen your ability to be Grateful for others!

SHARON
SARAGA WALTERS

Sharon has over 30 years experience operating and promoting her own businesses in **health and wellness,** and as co-owner of My Video Voice Productions, also serves as our administrative and marketing department.

She is the creator of Sharon it Forward Today on Facebook, and is a lifetime student and practitioner of Gratitude, with a passion for Sharing all good things. She's the lead creator of **The 28 Day Gratitude Workout** (TM), online course, book and workshop.

Sharon began her personal growth and awareness journey in 1989. She received a college degree in Health Promotions and spent 8 years as a Personal Fitness Trainer and owner of One to One Fitness. She has been a Licensed Massage Therapist for the past 25 years.

Facebook: www.facebook.com/The28DayGratitudeWorkout
www.facebook.com/sharonitforwardtoday
Website: www.the28daygratitudeworkout.com.

LOUANNE
SARAGA WALTERS

Louanne is a public speaker/moderator, Udemy instructor, co-founder of **My Video Voice Productions**, and co-producer and host of **The Philanthropy Show**®. She began working in radio in the mid 1980's learning all aspects of live and programmed radio broadcasting, and transitioned to television a few years later.

In addition to her behind the camera expertise, she's made the rare transition to 'on camera', capable of planning a project as producer, host, shooter and editor. Weaving video through multiple industries, she has been a news anchor/reporter, cruise director, financial advisor, and marketing and communications director.

She's *coached and mentored students* in video production, personal growth, finance, and organizational management over the past two and half decades, helping them discover, develop and deepen their talents and skill sets.

Facebook: www.facebook.com/LSaragaWalters
Twitter: @LouanneWalters
LinkedIn: www.linkedin.com/in/LouanneSaragaWalters

udemy

This workout is also available as an online video course via udemy.com. As an owner of The 28 Day Gratitude Workout book, we are pleased to offer you a special discount for the online course.

The online course includes:
- 33 video lectures, 2-3 min each
- Downloadable PDF's for each day's exercise
- Lifetime Access! Repeat the course as often as you like
- Or GIFT this course to a friend! Use the promo link below and select "GIFT THIS COURSE" in the dropdown box on sign-up.

The online course is regularly priced at $20, and is available to you for just $10 using this special discount code. Use coupon code BOOK10 or via this link: www.bit.ly/BOOK10.

Thank you!

Made in the USA
Charleston, SC
25 January 2017